Math Around Us

Car Math

Miguel Rosario

Cavendish
Square

New York

Published in 2015 by Cavendish Square Publishing, LLC
243 5th Avenue, Suite 136, New York, NY 10016

First Edition

Website: cavendishsq.com

This publication represents the opinions and views of the author based on his or her personal experience, knowledge, and research. The information in this book serves as a general guide only. The author and publisher have used their best efforts in preparing this book and disclaim liability rising directly or indirectly from the use and application of this book.

CPSIA Compliance Information: Batch #WW15CSQ

All websites were available and accurate when this book was sent to press.

Library of Congress Cataloging-in-Publication Data

Rosario, Miguel, author.
Car math / Miguel Rosario.
pages cm. — (Math around us)
Includes index.
ISBN 978-1-50260-149-0 (hardcover) ISBN 978-1-50260-156-8 (paperback) ISBN 978-1-50260-159-9 (ebook)
1. Arithmetic—Juvenile literature. 2. Counting—Juvenile literature. 3. Automobiles—Juvenile literature. I. Title.

QA115.R682 2015
513—dc23

2014025534

Editor: Amy Hayes
Copy Editor: Cynthia Roby
Art Director: Jeffrey Talbot
Designer: Douglas Brooks
Senior Production Manager: Jennifer Ryder-Talbot
Production Editor: David McNamaraa
Photo Researcher: J8 Media

Printed in the United States of America

Contents

There are **2** cars parked outside the **garage**.

Which car is bigger?

The grey car is bigger.

5

There are lots of cars in the **parking lot**.

How many cars are blue?

2 cars are blue.

This **school bus** has lots
of windows.

How many windows are on
the side of the bus?

10 windows are on the side
of the bus.

9

It is good to keep your car clean.

How many people are cleaning this car?

3 people are cleaning the car.

There are **3** cars parked on the street.

If **2** more parked on the street, how many cars would there be?

There would be **5** cars.

13

This isn't a car at all! This is a **motorcycle**.

How many **wheels** does a motorcycle have?

It has **2** wheels.

15

Jordan and his grandfather are fixing their car.

They have **1** of the **4** tools to fix their car.

How many more tools do they need?

They need **3** tools.

16

A car has **5** seats.

3 people get into the car.

How many seats are left?

2 seats are left.

19

1 white car drives away.

Cars and math sure are fun!

New Words

garage (gar-AJJ) A shelter to protect cars.

motorcycle (MO-tor-sy-cul) A vehicle with two wheels and a motor.

parking lot (PARK-ing LOT) An area where cars, trucks, and other vehicles park.

school bus (SKOOL BUS) A vehicle that takes children to and from school.

wheels (WEELS) Round objects attached to cars that allow them to move.

Index

About the Author

Miguel Rosario lives in Ellicottville, New York. He has two beautiful daughters and a great big dog named Elmo.

About

Bookworms help independent readers gain reading confidence through high-frequency words, simple sentences, and strong picture/text support. Each book explores a concept that helps children relate what they read to the world they live in.